W9-BVR-654

KINGS
&
QUEENS

KINGS & QUEENS

VICTOR DORFF

FALL RIVER PRESS

New York

FALL RIVER PRESS

New York

An Imprint of Sterling Publishing
387 Park Avenue South
New York, NY 10016

FALL RIVER PRESS and the distinctive Fall River Press logo are registered
trademarks of Barnes & Noble, Inc.

© 2013 by Fall River Press

All rights reserved. No part of this publication may be reproduced,
stored in a retrieval system, or transmitted in any form or by any means
(including electronic, mechanical, photocopying, recording, or otherwise)
without prior written permission from the publisher.

Cover design by Igor Satanovsky
Book design by Danielle Deschenes

ISBN 978-1-4351-4685-3

Distributed in Canada by Sterling Publishing
c/o Canadian Manda Group, 165 Dufferin Street
Toronto, Ontario, Canada M6K 3H6
Distributed in the United Kingdom by GMC Distribution Services
Castle Place, 166 High Street, Lewes, East Sussex, England BN7 1XU
Distributed in Australia by Capricorn Link (Australia) Pty. Ltd.
P.O. Box 704, Windsor, NSW 2756, Australia

For information about custom editions, special sales, and premium and
corporate purchases, please contact Sterling Special Sales at 800-805-5489 or
specialsales@sterlingpublishing.com.

Manufactured in Canada

2 4 6 8 10 9 7 5 3 1

www.sterlingpublishing.com

DEDICATION

To Lisa, the queen
of my realm.

INTRODUCTION

 hether it's a pivotal moment of history or a silly
episode of inappropriate, juvenile behavior, if
there's a member of the British royal family at
the center, the eyes of the world are glued on
Buckingham Palace.

But why?

It can't be the money. Lots of families are richer. Fame?
Pomp? Personality? Power? Probably not.

The secret to the popularity of the British monarchy is more
likely in the story itself—unique and ongoing.

The royal storyline is a combination of genres: historical
novel, epic legend, family drama, outrageous soap opera. We all
know the major plot-point touchstones: the Magna Carta, Henry
VIII and his wives, crazy King George III, prim and proper
Queen Victoria. The characters and history are familiar, but the
twists and turns have never stopped surprising us.

The English sovereigns also provide a treasure trove of
minutiae, from current information on *royal.gov.uk* to historical
tidbits still being unearthed in archaeological sites.

From the bedroom to the battlefields, the British royalty
have frightened us, amused us, awed us, and captivated our
imaginations for more than a thousand years.

The intent of this book is to keep that streak going just a little
longer.

Enjoy!

Why do so many countries around the world have Queen Elizabeth's likeness on their coins and stamps?

Queen Elizabeth is a lot more than just the queen of England.

Her official title is, "By the Grace of God, of the United Kingdom of Great Britain and Northern Ireland and of Her other Realms and Territories Queen, Head of the Commonwealth, Defender of the Faith."

Queen Elizabeth is actually the monarch of 15 other realms, in addition to the United Kingdom.

Each of those realms regards her as queen, which is why she is honored on their stamps and coins.

Does the queen have a different title in every one of her various realms?

Her official titles vary slightly, but there are some significant differences among different cultures.

In Britain, she is Lord of Man in the Isle of Man; Duke of Normandy in the Channel Islands; and Duke of Lancaster in the Duchy of Lancaster.

In the Maori language of native New Zealanders, the queen is known as Kotuku, which means "the white heron."

In Papua New Guinea, she is known in the pidgin language of Tok Pisin as "Missis Kwin," and as "Mama belong big family."

POP QUIZ

HIS SUBJECTS AROUND THE WORLD HAVE CALLED PRINCE CHARLES MANY THINGS. WHICH OF THESE IS *NOT* AMONG THE TITLES GIVEN TO HIM SINCE 2001?

    a. Nunavut—Son of the Big Boss

    b. New Zealand—Tall Man Riding Proud

    c. Saskatchewan—The Sun Looks at Him in a Good Way

    d. Tanzania—The Helper of the Cows

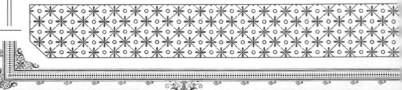

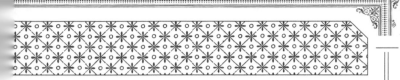

ANSWER: B.

New Zealand—Tall Man Riding Proud was not a title given to the Prince of Wales.

THE MANY CROWNS *of* THE BRITISH SOVEREIGN

The queen of England is the reigning monarch of these
16 Commonwealth realms, most of which are former
British colonies:

- Antigua and Barbuda
- Australia
- The Bahamas
- Barbados
- Belize
- Canada
- Grenada
- Jamaica
- New Zealand
- Papua New Guinea
- Saint Kitts and Nevis
- Saint Lucia
- Saint Vincent and the Grenadines
- Solomon Islands
- Tuvalu
- United Kingdom

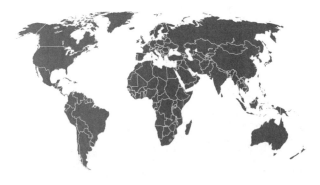

ADDITIONAL COUNTRIES IN THE COMMONWEALTH *of* NATIONS LED BY THE QUEEN

These nations are in addition to the 16 of which the queen is Head of State:

- Bangladesh
- Botswana
- Brunei
- Cameroon
- Cyprus
- Dominica
- Ghana
- Guyana
- India
- Kenya
- Kiribati
- Lesotho
- Malawi
- Malaysia
- Maldives
- Malta
- Mauritius
- Mozambique
- Namibia
- Nauru
- Nigeria
- Pakistan
- Samoa
- Seychelles
- Sierra Leone
- Singapore
- Solomon Islands
- South Africa
- Sri Lanka
- Swaziland
- Tanzania
- The Gambia
- Tonga
- Trinidad
- Uganda
- Vanuatu
- Zambia

Are England, Great Britain, and the United Kingdom the same?

No, but a lot of people get them confused. Great Britain is the combined kingdoms of England, Scotland, and Wales. It was officially created in 1707.

The United Kingdom (UK), formed in 1801, is Great Britain and the Irish Union combined. In 1921, most of Ireland became an independent republic, so it is no longer part of the UK, but Northern Ireland still is.

Things can get even more complicated than that, but don't worry… It's not going to be on the test. (Besides, there is no test.)

AMERICAN STATES
NAMED AFTER ENGLISH MONARCHS

- The Carolinas are named for King Charles I.

- Georgia is named for King George II.

- Maryland is named for Queen Henrietta Maria, wife of King Charles I.

- New York was named after the Duke of York, who later became King James II.

- Virginia and West Virginia are named for Queen Elizabeth I, the "Virgin Queen."

STATS

BUCKINGHAM PALACE

Buckingham Palace, the royal residence in London, has 775 rooms, including 19 State rooms, 52 royal and guest bedrooms, 188 staff bedrooms, 92 offices, and 78 bathrooms.

The palace is 354 feet long across the front, 394 feet deep (including the quadrangle), and 79 feet high. The total floor area of the Palace, from basement to roof, covers approximately 830,000 square feet.

Buckingham Palace's garden covers 40 acres.

STATS

THE ROYAL CORRESPONDENCE

During her reign, Queen Elizabeth II has…

- answered around three-and-a-half-million items of correspondence,

- sent more than 175,000 telegrams to congratulate people on living to be 100 years old,

- sent almost 540,000 telegrams to couples celebrating their 60th wedding anniversary,

- sent, with her husband, the Duke of Edinburgh, approximately 45,000 Christmas cards, and

- distributed approximately 90,000 Christmas puddings to staff.

STATS

CONGRATULATIONS FROM
QUEEN ELIZABETH II

The oldest person to receive a royal greeting was a 116-year-old Canadian man in 1984.

In 2006 and 2007, four sets of twins received royal congratulations for living a full century. (Incidentally, each twin received a slightly different greeting.)

The world's longest married couple, Mr. and Mrs. William Jones, received congratulations on their 83rd anniversary in 2006.

PERCY AND FLORENCE ARROWSMITH RECEIVED ROYAL GREETINGS FOR THEIR 60TH AND 70TH ANNIVERSARIES, PLUS INDIVIDUAL 100TH BIRTHDAY CARDS. MR. ARROWSMITH RECEIVED YET ANOTHER WHEN HE REACHED 105.

STATS

THE ROYAL TRAVELOGUE

Since ascending the throne, the queen has made 261 official overseas visits, including 96 State Visits, to 116 different countries.

Her first Commonwealth tour as queen (in 1954) included visits to Canada, Bermuda, Jamaica, Panama, Fiji, Tonga, New Zealand, Australia, the Cocos Islands, Ceylon, Aden, Uganda, Libya, Malta, and Gibraltar—covering a distance of 43,618 miles.

She has visited Australia 16 times, Canada 22 times, Jamaica six times, and New Zealand 10 times.

STATS

ROYAL HONORS AND PARTIES

Since 1952, the queen has conferred more than
404,500 honors and awards and personally held
more than 610 Investitures (the formal ceremony that
sometimes goes along with the honors).

Over the course of her reign, the queen has hosted
almost one-and-a-half-million people at garden
parties at Buckingham Palace and the Palace of
Holyroodhouse.

STATS

ROYAL COMPUTER RECYCLING

Since 2005, Computer Aid International helps the royal household ensure that old computer equipment is recycled or re-used in schools and community organizations, mainly in sub-Saharan Africa, including Kenya, Mali, Ethiopia, and Rwanda, but also in Asia and South America.

More than 2,392 pieces of computer equipment, including 726 monitors, 914 computers, and 47 laptops have been repurposed in this way.

Is Queen Elizabeth II related to *every* European monarch?

It certainly seems so. Queen Victoria is the great-great-grandmother of both King Juan Carlos of Spain and Queen Elizabeth II.

King Christian IX of Denmark is the great-great-grandfather of King Albert II of the Belgians, Queen Margrethe II of Denmark, King Harald V of Norway, and Queen Elizabeth II.

Willem IV, Prince of Orange, and Anne, Princess Royal of Great Britain (from the early 18th century), are the great-great-great-great-great grandparents of both Queen Beatrix of the Netherlands and Queen Elizabeth II.

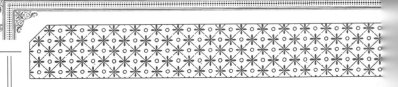

POP QUIZ

IN DECEMBER 2012, WHAT GIFT DID QUEEN ELIZABETH II'S MINISTERS GIVE HER TO COMMEMORATE HER 60 YEARS ON THE THRONE?

    a. A solid-gold stopwatch

    b. An electric toothbrush

    c. A set of placemats

    d. A rousing round of "For She's
       a Jolly Good Fellow"

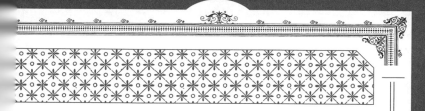

ANSWER: C.

The ministers gave the queen
60 placemats—one for each
year on the throne.

THE SAXON & DANISH KINGS

MONARCH	YEARS *of* REIGN
Egbert	802–839
Aethelwulf	839–858
Aethelbald	856–860
Aethelberht	860–865
Aethelred I	865–871
Alfred the Great	871–899
Edward the Elder	899–924
Athelstan	924–939
Edmund I	939–946
Eadred	946–955
Eadwig	955–959
Edgar the Peaceful	959–975
Edward the Martyr	975–978
Aethelred II, the Unready	978–1013
Sweyn I	1013–1014
Aethelred II, the Unready	1014–1016
Edmund Ironside	1016
Canute the Great	1016–1035
Harold I	1035–1040
Hardecanute	1040–1042
Edward the Confessor	1042–1066
Harold II	1066

ONLY ONE ENGLISH KING has been officially labeled "Great." Alfred, the Great, became King of Wessex in 871 AD, when he was 21 years old and the Vikings were attacking England.

Alfred succeeded in defending England against the Danes and establishing a network of town-fortresses called *burhs,* from which the word *borough* is derived.

King Alfred reached peace with the Danish Vikings, who continued to occupy parts of the north but were no longer a threat to his domain.

By the end of the ninth century, Alfred had begun to champion many intellectual pursuits and the unification of England as a country.

He learned Latin, so he could translate books to English (albeit a very *old* English).

He brought his country's finances under control, and he established a well-defined body of "Anglo-Saxon law."

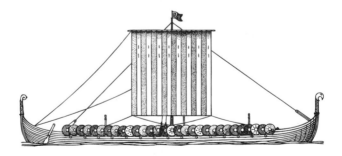

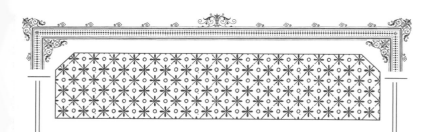

ALFRED'S SUCCESSORS, BEGINNING with King Edward the Elder, continued efforts to wrest England from Danish control for more than a hundred years, but they were ultimately unsuccessful.

By the early 11th century, the Danes in England were so overpowering that they no longer needed to fight the English to win their battles.

The English were willing to "buy" peace from the Danes by giving them thousands of pounds of silver.

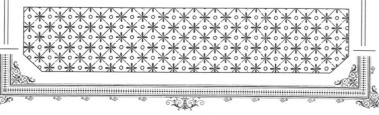

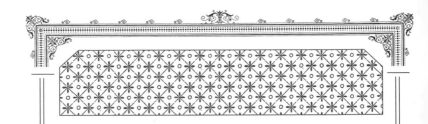

During the first 15 years of the 11th century, the Danes found *danegeld,* as the tribute was called, was much more profitable than ransacking the English countryside.

The English gave the Danes tons of silver to avoid armed conflict, until finally in 1016, Canute became the first Danish king of England.

By 1027, Canute was king of Britain, Denmark, Norway, and Sweden.

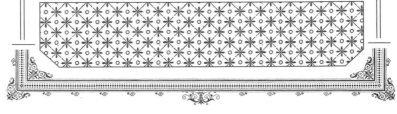

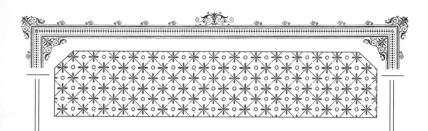

THE DANISH KINGS CONTINUED to reign over England until 1042, when King Hardecanute died childless at the age of 24.

Before his death, Hardecanute decided to call his Anglo-Saxon half-brother, Edward, back from exile in Normandy to make him heir to the throne.

Edward the Confessor ruled from 1042 to 1066, setting the stage for the end of Anglo-Saxon rule.

Edward the Confessor had spent 25 years in Normandy before becoming England's king, and that left him ill prepared to deal with his country's political landscape.

He married into the powerful English Godwine family shortly after taking the throne, but had a rocky relationship with the Godwines.

Edward's alliances in both England and Normandy ultimately created a serious conflict. At different times, he apparently promised two different people that they could be king when he died—and they both took him seriously.

HAROLD GODWINSON BELIEVED he had a solid claim to the throne because he was English and his family had, at times, supported King Edward during his reign.

William, Duke of Normandy, expected to become king of England in return for the protection he had given Edward before he became king.

Since Harold was on the scene when Edward the Confessor died, he assumed the role of king and served as the last of the Anglo-Saxon monarchs.

King Harold II led the Anglo-Saxons in a victorious march against the Norwegians who had captured York.

There, Harold's forces left little doubt that the days of Scandinavian rule in England were over.

But another invasion was already set in motion, and William of Normandy was about to become William the Conqueror.

THE NORMANS

MONARCH	YEARS *of* REIGN
William I, the Conqueror	1066–1087
William II, Rufus	1087–1100
Henry I	1100–1135
Stephen I	1135–1141
Empress Matilda	1141
Stephen I	1141–1154

William I, the Conqueror

WILLIAM THE CONQUEROR, leader of the Norman Invasion of 1066, was a descendant of the Vikings who had settled in Normandy.

In fact, the word Normandy has its roots in the French word *normand,* meaning Norseman, a person of the north.

William's victory launched a Norman rule of England that lasted nearly a century.

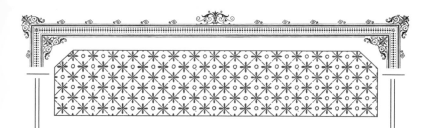

ON THE DAY OF HIS CORONATION, King William I promised that he would honor the existing laws and customs of the country he had just conquered.

For enforcement, however, he replaced the local sheriffs with his own men and established his own courts.

He also confiscated the land holdings of most of the English nobility, giving their estates to French-speaking allies who would provide William with needed military support.

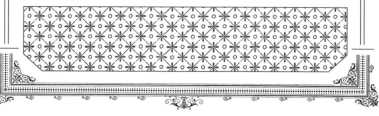

WILLIAM DECIDED IT WAS IMPORTANT to know exactly who and what he ruled after conquering England, so he could tax appropriately, among other things.

To find out, he began a comprehensive survey of all of England.

The scope of the review was so vast, it was called the Domesday Survey, drawing analogy to the final judgment at the end of the world (Doomsday).

The result is called the Domesday Book, and it is a record of everybody in the country *and* everything they owned.

ALTHOUGH ITS NAME IMPLIES a single, tall building, the Tower of London is actually a series of castles within castles.

The first construction was ordered by William the Conqueror, who commissioned the White Tower—a stone castle designed to intimidate Londoners and provide protection against invaders.

It was finished in 1097.

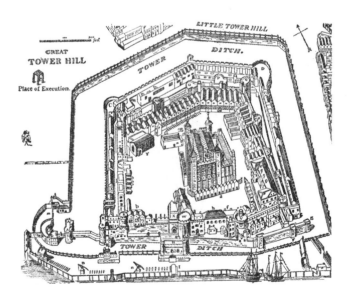

STATS

THE TOWER OF LONDON

Since the time of William the Conqueror, subsequent British monarchs have built another 20 towers as part of the Tower of London.

The entire complex now covers 18 acres of the capital city and is an official UNESCO World Heritage site.

OFFICIAL RESIDENCES *of* QUEEN ELIZABETH II

- Buckingham Palace has been the official London home of the sovereign since 1837.

- Windsor Castle, the largest occupied castle in the world, is more than 900 years old.

- The Palace of Holyroodhouse was built in 1128 as a monastery, but today is the official royal residence in Scotland.

- Balmoral Castle is Queen Elizabeth's private residence in Scotland.

- Sandringham House has been a private home for the British royal family since 1862.

- St. James's Palace is not open to the public.

- Kensington Palace is the birthplace of Queen Victoria and still serves as a royal residence.

CURRENTLY UNOCCUPIED ROYAL RESIDENCES

- ◆ Hampton Court Palace was home to King Henry VIII.

- ◆ The Tower of London became the home of the Crown Jewels of the United Kingdom in 1303.

- ◆ The Banqueting House was once part of Whitehall Palace, where King Charles I was executed.

- ◆ Kew Palace was home for King George III in his later years.

- ◆ Allerton Castle is the former home to Prince Frederick Augustus, "The Grand Old Duke of York."

- ◆ Audley End House was purchased by King Charles II, but when the house needed major repairs, King William III gave it back.

- ◆ New Hall (or the Palace of Beaulieu) is the home of a school and the Royal Arms of Henry VIII.

- ◆ Cambridge Cottage is also known as Kew Gardens Gallery.

- ◆ Carisbrooke Castle, on the Isle of Wight, was "home" to King Charles I, because he was imprisoned there for more than a year before his execution.

For more than 700 years, the Tower of London has been locked each night with the "Ceremony of the Keys."

A limited number of visitors from the public are allowed to accompany the "Chief Yeoman Warder of the Tower" and the "Escort of the Key" as they travel from gate to gate, securing the Tower for the night and making sure the Crown Jewels are safe.

STATS

ROYAL GUN SALUTES

The number of rounds fired in a royal salute depends on the place and occasion. The basic royal salute is 21 rounds. In Hyde Park an extra 20 rounds are added because it is a royal park.

At the Tower of London 62 rounds are fired on royal anniversaries (the basic 21, plus a further 20 because the Tower is a royal palace and fortress, plus another 21 "for the City of London") and 41 on other occasions.

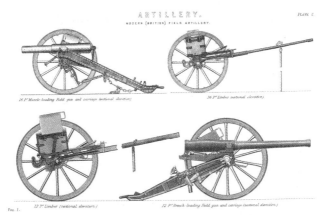

The Tower of London became the home of exotic wild animals in 1210, during the reign of King John.

Starting with lions, bears, and elephants, the royal menagerie grew over time to include a vast array of animals from around the world.

For example, in 1764, George III received a cheetah from India, and in 1827, George IV received a giraffe from Egypt.

In the 1830s, all the animals—including alligators, monkeys, and snakes—were transferred to the newly created London Zoo.

POP QUIZ

THE ROYAL FAMILY INTRODUCED A NEW BREED OF DOG WHEN THE QUEEN'S CORGI MATED WITH HER SISTER'S PET.

Which of these was the royal formula?

a. Corgi + Poodle = Poogi

b. Corgi + Spaniel = Sporgi

c. Corgi + Bulldog = Burgi

d. Corgi + Dachshund = Dorgi

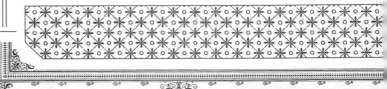

ANSWER: D.

Princess Margaret's dog, Pipkin,
was a Dachshund. There have
now been 10 royal Dorgis:
Tinker, Pickles, Chipper, Piper,
Harris, Brandy, Berry, Cider,
Candy, and Vulcan.

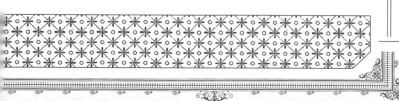

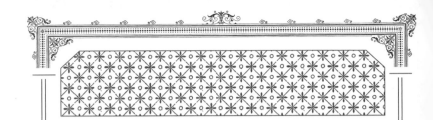

WHEN WILLIAM WON ENGLAND in his victory at the Battle of Hastings in 1066, he became ruler of both England and parts of northern France.

When he died in 1087, one son, Robert, inherited Normandy and another son, William II, became king of England.

This division set the stage for fights over control of northern France that lasted for hundreds of years.

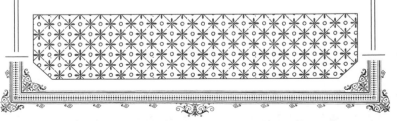

WILLIAM II REPORTEDLY BROUGHT an effeminate sense of fashion to his royal court.

A contemporary critic complained of the flowing hair and extravagant dress that became a popular sign of the time.

In addition, shoes with curved points at the toes were reportedly an uncomfortable, but ubiquitous invention of the era.

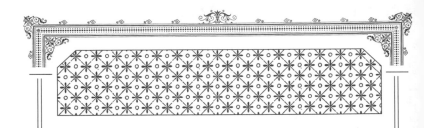

WILLIAM II WAS CALLED William Rufus (or William the Red). The name referred to the color of his hair and complexion, and probably wasn't used to describe the king until after his death.

William Rufus died while hunting in the New Forest, when he was shot in the back with an arrow.

Accident? Perhaps. No one knows, but many believe he was murdered.

Today, the Rufus Stone stands where William II fell.

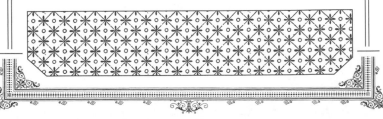

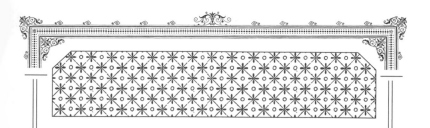

On the death of William II in 1100, his brother Henry took the throne and immediately began solidifying his support, anticipating a conflict with their brother Robert, who still ruled Normandy.

King Henry I made friends quickly by promising to end the heavy taxes, confiscation of church property, and other excesses that had made William II unpopular.

KING HENRY I HAD NO male heirs at his death, so he named his daughter Matilda as his heir.

At the time of Henry's death, however, Matilda was married to the Holy Roman Emperor and was living on the Continent.

With Matilda out of the way, her cousin Stephen— nephew of Henry I and grandson of William the Conqueror—took the crown in 1135, even though he had promised to recognize cousin Matilda as England's rightful ruler.

Matilda's followers immediately began the fight against King Stephen on her behalf, and it was still going on when she arrived in England with an army in 1139.

At one point, in 1141, Stephen was taken prisoner and Matilda prepared to take over as England's first queen.

She went to London expecting to be coronated, but the public rebelled and forced her to flee the city.

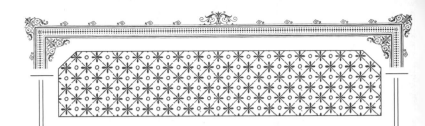

STEPHEN DIDN'T REMAIN Matilda's prisoner for very long. His army arranged a prisoner swap, and the civil war continued until 1153.

Under the terms of a peace treaty, Stephen remained king of England, but he agreed that Matilda's son Henry would be the next king.

When Stephen died in 1154, Henry II took over, ending the reign of the Norman kings.

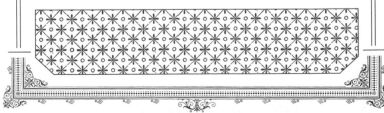

THE PLANTAGENETS

MONARCH	YEARS *of* REIGN
Henry II	1154–1189
Richard I "the Lionheart"	1189–1199
John I	1199–1216
Henry III	1216–1272
Edward I	1272–1307
Edward II	1307–1327
Edward III	1327–1377
Richard II	1377–1399

Richard II

Henry II controlled England and a large portion of France, and his method of ruling involved a lot of travel.

He is probably best remembered for his personal conflict with Thomas Becket.

Thinking the move would expand his power, Henry named his friend Becket as Archbishop of Canterbury, but Becket took the assignment seriously.

After Henry expressed frustration over Becket's resistance to his authority, four knights assassinated the Archbishop.

Henry II blamed himself for the murder and consented to orders from the Pope to do penance.

COMMON LAW LEGAL PRINCIPLES
CREDITED TO HENRY II

- A system that gave grand juries the power to name criminal suspects to be tried.

- Property rights secured by rules that allowed individuals to exchange ownership of land.

- Rules of inheritance granting the eldest son control of his father's estate.

- Local courts with 12-man juries to settle simple land disputes and royal courts where criminal cases were tried by the king's justices.

RICHARD THE LIONHEART was king of England for 10 years, but he barely spent 10 months of that time in the country, and he didn't speak the language.

To him, being king was just a way to finance the Crusades he wanted to fight in the Holy Land.

He is said to have been willing to sell London, itself, if he could find someone rich enough to pay for it.

KING RICHARD'S BROTHER and successor, King John, is best remembered for having made his barons mad enough to force him to sign the Magna Carta in 1215, then reneging on the promises it contained as soon as he could.

His opponents invited a French prince to come take the throne, which triggered an invasion.

King John died while fighting to keep his kingdom.

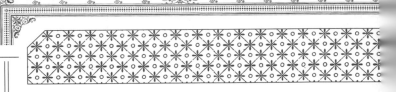

POP QUIZ

Who was Solomon Attefeld?

a. First Chancellor of the Exchequer under King Henry VII

b. The given name of the man who became King Aethelred II, the Unready

c. The Royal Head-Holder for King John, who suffered from seasickness

d. The best man at the wedding of former King Edward VIII to Wallis Simpson

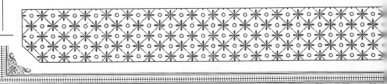

ANSWER: C.

Solomon Attefeld was the Royal
Head-Holder who accompanied
King John on all his sea voyages.

THE HOUSES OF LANCASTER & YORK

MONARCH	YEARS *of* REIGN
Henry IV	1399–1413
Henry V	1413–1422
Henry VI	1422–1461
Edward IV	1461–1470
Henry VI	1470–1471
Edward IV	1471–1483
Edward V	1483
Richard III	1483–1485

Lancaster Rose   *York Rose*   *Tudor Rose*

THE NAME "WAR OF THE ROSES" belies the violence and animosity behind the civil war that gripped England from 1455 to 1485.

The Yorks and the Lancasters represented two branches of the same royal family, descendants of King Edward III, and they were locked in a struggle for control of the country.

The one group wore an emblem with a red rose. The other wore a white rose.

WHEN HENRY TUDOR WAS BORN, his father was already dead, his mother was 14 years old, and he was destined to be the last hope of the Lancasters.

A rift had formed among the ruling Yorks, when King Richard III wrested the throne from the young sons of his brother, Edward V.

Edward's widow and Henry's mom made a deal: If Henry became king, he would marry Edward's surviving daughter, Elizabeth. They would create a merger of the two factions *and* a new family emblem with a red and white rose.

Thorny problem solved.

IN 1485, AT THE BATTLE OF BOSWORTH FIELD, King Richard III became the last English king to die in battle.

His crown was placed on the head of the 28-year-old Henry Tudor, and a dynasty was born.

Richard's body was stripped, tossed over the back of a horse, and publicly humiliated as it was carried to the nearby town.

And King Henry VII rode triumphantly to take the throne.

HENRY TUDOR PUT THE CORPSE of King Richard III on public display for two days, to eliminate any possibility of a pretender someday claiming to be the former king.

Richard's body was buried without ceremony in a local Franciscan churchyard.

The exact location had been forgotten, until September 2012.

That's when archaeologists digging in a parking lot in Leicester, England, said they had discovered the site of the Franciscan church *and* a skeleton they thought might be Richard III's.

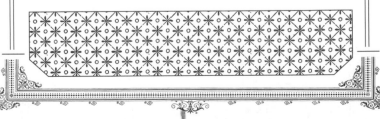

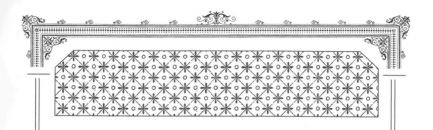

THE SKELETAL REMAINS FOUND under the Leicester parking lot were subjected to a series of carbon-dating tests and compared to DNA samples taken from known descendants of King Richard III's sister, Anne of York.

In February 2013, scientists announced that the skeleton was, indeed, that of the last English king to die in battle, and that he would be laid to rest, once again.

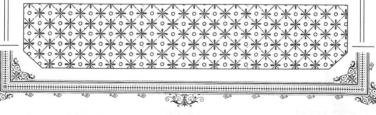

THE HOUSE OF TUDOR

MONARCH	YEARS *of* REIGN
Henry VII	1485–1509
Henry VIII	1509–1547
Edward VI	1547–1553
Lady Jane Grey	1553
Mary I	1553–1558
Elizabeth I	1558–1603

Henry VIII

King Henry VII chose a wife for his first-born son, Arthur, when the child was three years old.

In 1501, when Arthur was 13, he was married by proxy to Princess Catherine of Aragon, with the Spanish ambassador acting as stand-in for the bride.

Arthur and his bride wrote to each other in Latin for two years before they finally met.

They were quite surprised to find that they could not understand each other, because they had each learned a different pronunciation of the dead language they had in common.

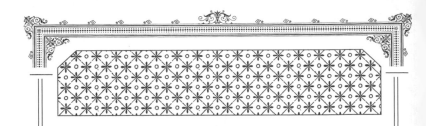

WITHIN A MATTER OF MONTHS of his marriage, Prince Arthur had died of a disease called the sweating sickness, and his younger brother Henry became the heir-apparent.

Not only was the young Prince Henry quickly prepared for his future role as king, but also arrangements were made for him to marry his brother's widow so the alliance with Spain would not be lost.

That is how Catherine of Aragon came to be the first of the many wives of King Henry VIII.

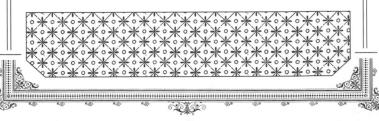

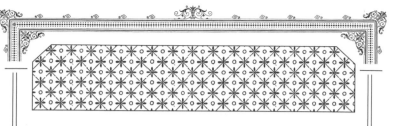

In 1520, HENRY VIII and the French King Francis I met in friendship on neutral ground between their countries.

Both nations went all out in their efforts to impress the other with riches and splendor.

Embroidered carpets and cloth made of gold thread and jewels were used to create a literal "Field of the Cloth of Gold" for the occasion.

Contemporaries called the decked-out meeting site the eighth wonder of the world.

By the end of the 18-day spectacle, when everyone headed home, Henry VIII was running out of money.

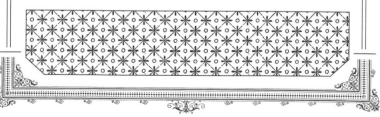

STATS

THE ROYAL SWAG

By the end of his reign, King Henry VIII had 55 palaces, 2,000 tapestries, 150 paintings, and nearly 1,800 books.

He also owned 41 gowns, 25 doublets (buttoned jackets), 20 coats, eight cloaks, 15 capes, and eight walking sticks.

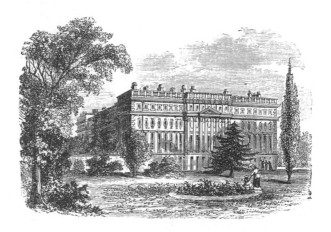

STATS

THE KITCHENS OF HENRY VIII

King Henry VIII expanded the kitchens in his Hampton Court Palace to include 55 rooms covering 3,000 square feet.

Two hundred people worked to provide 600 meals, twice a day, to feed the royal court.

Records for one year during the time of the Tudors show that the total wild animal consumption was 1,240 oxen, 8,200 sheep, 2,330 deer, 760 calves, 1,870 pigs, and 53 wild boar.

And to drink?

600,000 gallons of ale.

In 1521, Pope Leo X gave King Henry VIII the title "Defender of the Faith" to thank him for his defense of the Roman Catholic Church against Martin Luther's Protestant movement.

In the next decade, after the Pope famously refused to grant the king permission to divorce his first wife, Catherine, Henry VIII severed his ties with the Roman Catholic Church and declared himself the "Supreme Governor of the Church of England."

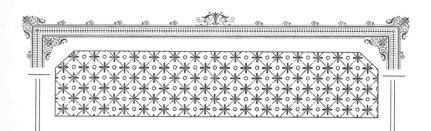

TODAY, "DEFENDER OF THE FAITH" is still part of the official title of the British monarch, but Prince Charles has said that he is looking forward to changing that.

When he becomes king, Charles says he wants a designation that better reflects the diversity of religions practiced by his subjects—perhaps, "Defender of the Faiths" or "Defender of Faith."

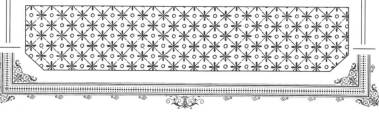

THE GROWTH OF PROTESTANTISM in England was an unintended consequence of Henry VIII's pursuit of a male heir.

Although he rejected the supremacy of the Roman Pope, Henry VIII never approved of the teachings of Martin Luther and continued to think of himself as Catholic.

Becoming the supreme leader of the Church of England was Henry VIII's only way of freeing himself to divorce and to marry women at will.

THE SIX WIVES *of* HENRY VIII
AND WHAT HAPPENED TO THEM

Catherine of Aragon	1509–1533	Divorced
Anne Boleyn	1533–1536	Executed
Jane Seymour	1536–1537	Died
Anne of Cleves	1540	Divorced
Kathryn Howard	1540–1542	Executed
Katherine Parr	1543–1547	Widowed

ANNE BOLEYN.   JANE SEYMOUR.   KATHARINE HOWARD.

THE CLOTHES ANNE BOLEYN wore to hide some of her physical features are said by some to have wound up influencing fashion in the court of King Henry VIII.

The long, hanging sleeves she reportedly wore to cover up an imperfection on her hand became popular during the era.

The embroidered choker she may have worn to hide a mole was also imitated by the women of the court.

WHEN HENRY VIII DIED, he was buried next to his third wife, Jane Seymour, who was the mother of his only son, who became King Edward VI.

Edward VI was the first English monarch raised as a Protestant.

He was crowned at the age of nine and never made it to adulthood.

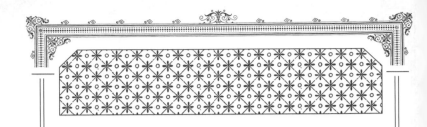

THE FAIR COMPLEXION of the young King Edward VI was the envy of many men in his court.

In fact, it is said that his pale skin became such a fashion statement that some men endured blood-letting two or three times a year to get just the right shade of skin tone.

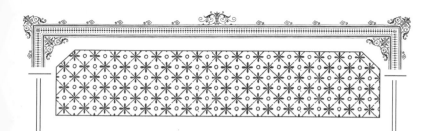

AT THE AGE OF 15, Edward VI knew he was dying.

His Catholic sister Mary was next in line for the throne, and he did not want to let that happen.

The dying king ordered that his cousin Lady Jane Grey should be made queen upon his death, but he was not doing her any favor.

Jane's reign lasted nine days and ended with her execution as Mary and the Catholics regained control of England.

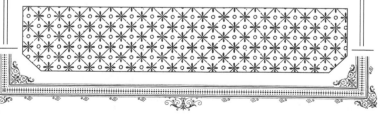

Queen Mary I was England's first Queen Regnant—one who ruled by her own right, rather than by virtue of marrying a king.

Hers was a reign of terror, as she killed hundreds of Protestants as part of a ruthless campaign to restore Catholicism as England's national religion.

For her efforts, she became known as "Bloody Mary."

WHEN MARY DIED AT THE AGE OF 42, her Protestant half-sister Elizabeth was next in line for the throne.

During her reign, Queen Elizabeth I helped forge a compromise that quieted the conflict between Catholics and Protestants.

That compromise was articulated in the 39 Articles of 1563, which is still referred to as a foundation of faith in the Church of England.

Why was Queen Elizabeth I able to reduce the tensions that seemed to be growing so violently between the two religions of her realm?

Elizabeth was able to rise above the differences, in part, because she saw the Protestants and Catholics as more alike than different.

"I have no desire to make windows into men's souls," Elizabeth said. "There is only one Christ, Jesus… only one faith. All else is a dispute over trifles."

Did Queen Elizabeth I lead her troops in battle against the Spanish Armada?

No. The Spanish never arrived, but, while they were on their way, Queen Elizabeth joined her troops, ready to fight, telling them:

"… I am come … in the midst and heat of the battle, to live or die amongst you all; to lay down, for my God, and for my kingdom, and for my people, my honor and my blood, even the dust. I know I have but the body of a weak and feeble woman; but I have the heart of a king, and of a king of England, too…"

Was Queen Elizabeth I *really*
a virgin queen?

Given everything we know about the behavior that was so common in the royal courts of her era, probably not.

Elizabeth certainly had her favorites, but ruling over a husband might have proved even more difficult at the time than ruling over a nation.

What we know is that she never married and never had children.

She died with no heirs, so the reign of the Tudors ended with her.

Instead, the crown went to James Stuart, a distant cousin and great-great-grandson of Henry VIII's sister.

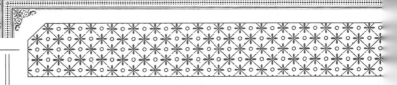

POP QUIZ

WHICH ENGLISH MONARCH WAS THE FIRST TO TAX TOBACCO OUT OF CONCERN FOR THE DAMAGE IT DOES TO THE LUNGS?

    a. Queen Elizabeth I, in 1602

    b. King James I, in 1604

    c. Queen Victoria, in 1847

    d. King George VI, in 1932

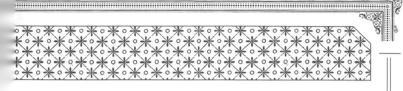

ANSWER: B.

King James I called smoking, "hateful to the nose, harmful to the brain, and dangerous to the lungs."

THE HOUSE *of* STUART

MONARCH	YEARS *of* REIGN
James I	1603–1625
Charles I	1625–1649
Commonwealth of England	1649–1660
Charles II	1660–1685
James II	1685–1688
William III / Mary II	1689–1702
Anne	1702–1714

JAMES I

JAMES STUART WAS CROWNED King James VI of Scotland when he was only one year old.

When he became King James I of England and Ireland at the age of 36, in 1603, he was the first person to rule over all three countries.

King James I gave his domain the name "Great Britain."

KING JAMES I WAS THE SON of the Catholic Mary, Queen of Scots, but he was raised as a Protestant.

The policies of James I, however, angered supporters of both religions.

Protestants resisted his efforts to encourage trade with Spain, a Catholic country.

A group of domestic Catholics attempted to blow up King James I and the Parliament in the failed Gunpowder Plot.

On November 4, 1605, Guy Fawkes was caught in the House of Lords with enough gunpowder to destroy the building.

The failure of this plot to kill King James I and destroy the Parliament is still celebrated in England on November 5 as Guy Fawkes Day.

Festivities include bonfires, fireworks, and the burning of Fawkes in effigy.

The effigies are called "guys," and today's use of the word "guy" as a generic reference to people is a remnant of the memory of Guy Fawkes.

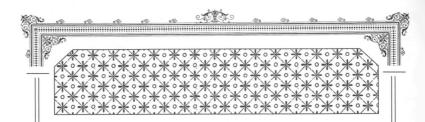

To THIS DAY, the Gunpowder Plot is memorialized in a series of traditions that take place before the queen attends the ceremonial "Opening of Parliament."

First, a detachment of guards is sent by the queen to search the cellars of both houses of Parliament, looking for evidence of any evil plots.

Then, a "hostage" member of Parliament is brought to Buckingham Palace to guarantee the safe return of the monarch.

Only then does the queen travel to the House of Lords for the opening ceremonies.

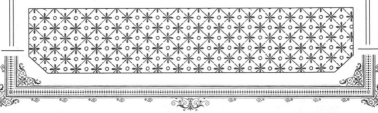

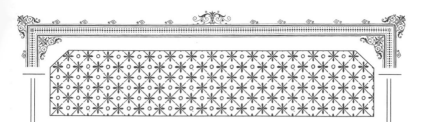

KING JAMES I commissioned the King James Bible
and believed fervently in the "Divine Right of Kings"
to rule their subjects.

His bible went on to become a standard—"the most
printed book in the world."

His philosophy of government put him in direct
conflict with Parliament, which held the purse strings
and made it difficult for the king to raise money.

ALTHOUGH KING JAMES I was married to Anne, the daughter of the King of Denmark, for 30 years and had eight children with her, he is better known for his relationships with other men.

In fact, a popular saying at the time was, "Elizabeth was King; now James is Queen."

As the 13-year-old king of Scotland, James met Esmé Stewart, a 37-year-old relative, and made him the first Duke of Lennox.

Upset by the personal relationship between the two men, the Scottish nobles kidnapped the king and held him prisoner for 10 months, until the king agreed to banish the Duke of Lennox to France.

AFTER QUEEN ANNE'S DEATH in 1619, King James I met and fell in love with George Villiers, whom he made Duke of Buckingham.

The relationship lasted until King James's death in 1625.

Buckingham was assassinated three years later and is buried in Westminster Abbey, in a tomb adjacent to that of King James.

Was King James I open about his sexual relationships with men?

 Yes. King James I referred to the Duke of Buckingham as "my wife and child" and defended his choice of lover in a speech to the Privy Council:

"…I love the Earl of Buckingham more than anyone else… I wish to speak in my own behalf and not to have it thought to be a defect, for Jesus Christ did the same, and therefore I cannot be blamed. Christ had John, and I have George."

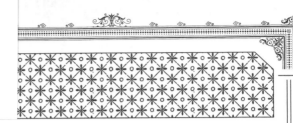

Upon the death of King James I, King Charles I ascended to the throne in 1625.

Like his father, King Charles believed in the supremacy of the crown over its subjects.

He dissolved the Parliament and was absolute ruler until 1640, when the legislature reappeared and passed a law saying it couldn't be dissolved without its own consent.

This set the stage for civil war in England.

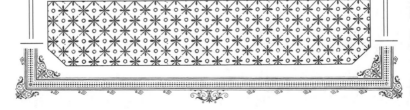

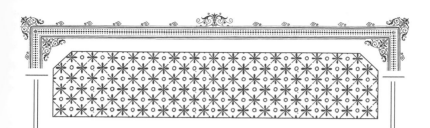

IN 1642, AFTER KING CHARLES I tried and failed to arrest members of Parliament, he was forced to leave London and declared war on the legislature.

The civil war culminated in victory for Parliament, the beheading of the king, and the beginning of the first British Commonwealth, which was led by Puritan Oliver Cromwell.

Cromwell was offered the crown, but refused it, so he doesn't really belong in a book about kings and queens.

Was democracy a prominent
feature of the first British
Commonwealth?

No. Although the monarchy was abolished and there was discussion about creating a new representative body to govern, it never happened.

In fact, Oliver Cromwell became so fed up with the continuing gyrations of Parliament, he dissolved it himself in 1653, essentially making himself the dictator.

After his death, pro-Royalist forces gradually brought back a constitutional monarchy to rule England.

In 1660, THE MONARCHY was restored in England with the coronation of King Charles II, who ended Puritanical rule.

The Restoration facilitated the re-opening of theatres, the resurgence of interest in science, the flight of Puritans to the New World… and a return of the tug-of-war between Protestants and Catholics for control of England.

IN 1670, KING CHARLES II signed a secret pact with France called the Treaty of Dover.

Charles II promised that he would support France's military in an effort to subjugate the Dutch *and* he would convert himself and his country to Catholicism.

In return, France would provide the king of England with enough money to make him independent of Parliament.

France's King Louis XIV only cared about war, and Britain's King Charles II thought switching to Catholicism would make it easier for him to be absolute ruler.

Since neither of the two men really cared very much about religion, the religious conversion clause of the secret Treaty of Dover was never implemented.

IN 1673, PARLIAMENT FORCED King Charles II to sign the Test Act, making it illegal for Catholics to hold office.

By 1679, the money from France had given Charles the independence he needed to allow him to dissolve Parliament and prevent the passage of the Exclusion Act, which would have taken his brother James (and all other Catholics) out of the line of succession to the throne.

Charles II waited until he was on his deathbed to become a Catholic.

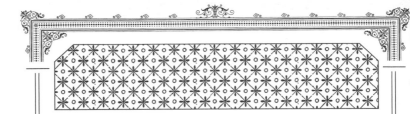

KING CHARLES II, a notorious womanizer, is
remembered as the "Merry Monarch."

His court was said to have resembled a brothel.

He had at least 14 illegitimate children by at least
eight different women.

In fact, many of the dukes, marquises, and earls in
modern-day England are direct descendants of the
Merry Monarch and his mistresses.

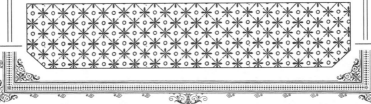

STATS

ROYAL BASTARDS

*An incomplete list of British monarchs
and the number of illegitimate children
they are **known** to have fathered:*

Henry I:	22
Charles II:	14
John:	7
Henry II:	4
George III:	4
Stephen:	2
Henry VIII:	2
Richard I:	1

If I am a descendant of the illegitimate offspring of British royalty, what should I do about it?

There is a venerable organization that might welcome
you as a member: The Descendants of the Illegitimate
Sons and Daughters of the Kings of Britain
(*www.royalbastards.org*).

Founded in 1961 by a member of the American
Society of Genealogists, its qualification for
membership is simple: prove you are descended
from an illegitimate child of a king, of an illegitimate
child of a child of a king, or an illegitimate child of
a grandchild of a king, of England, Scotland, Wales,
Great Britain, or the United Kingdom.

THE PERSONAL MOTTO of King Charles II reportedly was, "God will never damn a man for allowing himself a little pleasure."

About this same time, however, syphilis had begun sweeping through Europe.

This confluence of events brought about the popular use of early condoms, which were made of fish skins and were intended not for contraception, but for the prevention of disease.

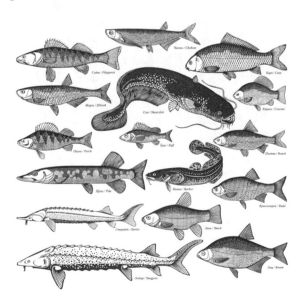

KING CHARLES II TOOK the daughter of the king of Portugal as a wife, along with an enormous cash dowry, naval bases in Tangiers and Bombay, and South American trading privileges.

Charles married Princess Catherine of Braganza twice—once in a secret Catholic ceremony, then publicly by an Anglican priest.

Marriage did not stop the king from having a string of mistresses and fathering illegitimate children, but he showed his loyalty to Catherine in other ways.

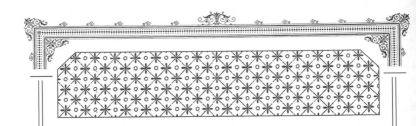

QUEEN CATHERINE WAS not popular in the court of King Charles II.

Her English was poor, she was unable to provide an heir to the throne, and she was devoutly Catholic during a time of intense anti-Catholic sentiment.

Charles rejected all advice to divorce Catherine or to legitimize one of his bastard sons, saying that he would not abandon her and "I will not see an innocent woman abused."

They remained married until Charles's death in 1685.

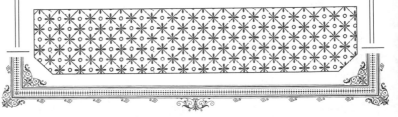

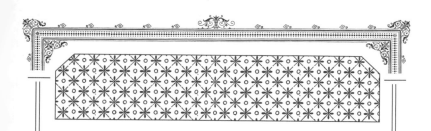

For seven years after the death of King Charles II, Queen Dowager Catherine remained in England, where she was barely tolerated.

She repeatedly asked her brother, the king of Portugal, to allow her to return home, but he refused.

Finally, in 1693, permission was granted, and the public gave her a hero's welcome when she arrived.

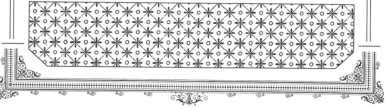

CATHERINE, THE ENGLISH QUEEN DOWAGER, spent many happy years of retirement in a palace with a chapel outside of Lisbon.

Then, in 1704, she was declared regent until her nephew became of age to succeed his father as king of Portugal.

Catherine of Braganza ruled Portugal well until her death in 1705, when she was given a monarch's funeral.

Although English history remembers Queen Catherine as unremarkable, Catherine of Braganza is remembered with the greatest respect in her native country today.

KING CHARLES II WAS SUCCEEDED by his brother James who had scandalously married a commoner, Anne Hyde.

They had seven children, but only two survived— Mary and Anne.

Although the kids were raised as Protestants, James converted to Catholicism while in exile in France during the time of the first English Commonwealth.

On the death of his wife, James married a 15-year-old Italian Catholic princess.

THE RELIGION OF KING JAMES II and his wife, combined with his belief in Divine rule, did not ingratiate him with his subjects.

He survived several attempts at rebellion as he worked to restore Catholic rule in England.

When his young wife gave birth to a potential heir, however, the public revolt was unstoppable.

PRINCESS MARY, THE PROTESTANT daughter of King James II by his first wife, Anne Hyde, had married her Protestant cousin William, the grandson of King Charles I.

William was invited by the English nobility to invade and to overthrow their Catholic king, to restore Protestantism and democracy to the land.

William agreed and launched an invasion that came in unopposed by the Royal Navy.

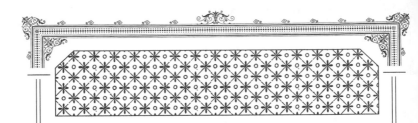

WHEN PRINCE WILLIAM OF ORANGE began his march on London, thousands of locals joined his army to retake the country, in what came to be known as the "Glorious Revolution."

On the way, William was joined by Anne, the other Protestant daughter of King James II, and John (an ancestor of Winston) Churchill.

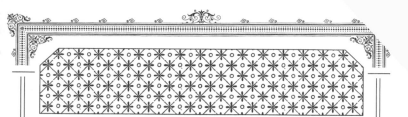

IN THE FACE OF THE POPULAR Protestant uprising that included two of his daughters, King James II ran away to France.

His daughter was declared Queen Mary II, but she insisted she would only take the job if her husband ruled jointly as King William III.

William and Mary were the only royal couple to rule England jointly.

KING WILLIAM III and Queen Mary II, Parliament passed a Bill of Rights, designed to undo many of the actions of King James II and to limit royal powers.

Now, Catholics could no longer be sovereigns.

Kings and queens could not withhold laws passed by Parliament, nor could they impose taxes without legislative consent.

In succeeding years, the Bank of England was formed to control spending, and the Act of Settlement of 1701 was passed to strengthen the Bill of Rights.

THE HOUSES OF PARLIAMENT.

Interior of the House of Lords.

UNDER THE ACT OF SETTLEMENT of 1701, the sovereign was no longer free to declare war or leave the country without Parliamentary approval.

An independent judiciary was created, because judges could no longer be removed without good cause.

The monarch was required to swear to maintain the Church of England.

More specifically, the crown could not pass to a Catholic *or* to anyone who married a Catholic.

In addition, only Protestant heirs of Sophia of Hanover, a granddaughter of King James I, were eligible to rule.

MANY OF THE RULES established by the Act of Settlement of 1701 still apply to the royal family. For example, both the Earl of St. Andrews and HRH Prince Michael of Kent lost the right of succession to the throne by marrying Catholics.

Their children, however, can still inherit the crown, as long as they are "in communion with the Church of England."

AFTER THE DEATHS OF William and Mary, Mary's sister Anne became the last of the monarchs of the Stuart dynasty.

Queen Anne was married to Prince George of Denmark, who was, by all accounts a wholly unremarkable man.

As her uncle, King Charles II put it, "I have tried him drunk and I have tried him sober, and there is nothing in him."

Nevertheless, Anne was pregnant by Prince George at least 17 times.

None of her children survived into adulthood, however, so she did not produce an heir.

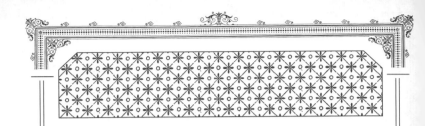

During the reign of Queen Anne, the United Kingdom of Great Britain was created in 1707, when Scotland was officially joined with England.

During the War of the Spanish Succession, John Churchill, Duke of Marlborough, won significant military victories in the name of Queen Anne.

Meanwhile, Churchill's wife, Sarah, was said to be extremely influential in the Royal Court.

Sarah's memoirs, published decades after the death of the Queen, imply that she and Anne had been lovers.

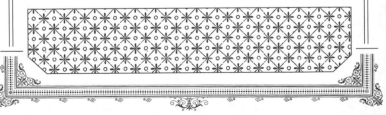

THE HOUSE *of* HANOVER

MONARCH	YEARS *of* REIGN
George I	1714–1727
George II	1727–1760
George III	1760–1820
George IV	1820–1830
William IV	1830–1837
Victoria	1837–1901

SOPHIA OF HANOVER, granddaughter of King James I, was born in the Netherlands.

Even though she never set foot in England, the Act of Succession of 1701 made her next in line for the throne after Queen Anne.

Unfortunately for Sophia, however, she died two months before Queen Anne, so the title passed to Sophia's son, King George I.

This ended the rule of the House of Stuart and began the era of the House of Hanover.

AT THE TIME OF Queen Anne's death, King George I
was 52nd in line to the throne, but he was Protestant…
and that was enough to bump him up to Number One
under the Settlement Act.

George was born and raised in Hanover, Germany, and
spoke no English when he became king, and at the age
of 54, he saw no particular reason to learn it.

He had come to England primarily for the money.

IN ORDER TO SPEND more time at home in Hanover, King George I persuaded Parliament to repeal the law that limited his ability to leave the country.

In return, he left most of the details of running the government to his ministers, with whom he communicated in French.

Among those ministers, Sir Robert Walpole emerged as the leader and was named first lord of the treasury and chancellor of the exchequer.

More about him later…

In his youth, George I married his cousin Sophia Dorothea of Celle, and they had two children.

In 1694, 20 years before he became king of England, George found out that Sophia had had an affair.

He divorced her and imprisoned her in a German castle, where she remained for more than 30 years, until her death in 1726.

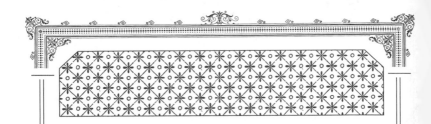

When George I arrived in England to take on the role of king, he brought along 18 cooks and two mistresses.

One of the mistresses was tall and thin (known as the Maypole), while the other was short and fat (referred to as Elephant and Castle).

The public did not take kindly to the German George, his mistresses, or the rumors about how he had treated his wife.

He spent most of his time out of the country. He died at his home in Hanover in 1727.

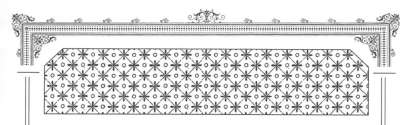

LIKE HIS FATHER, King George II was also born and grew up in Hanover, Germany, and he liked to go back regularly.

Also like his father, he relied heavily on his ministers to run the government for him.

Sir Robert Walpole had survived the transition from George the father to George the son, essentially becoming the first prime minister, although the title did not yet exist.

In fact, in 1735, King George II gave Walpole 10 Downing Street as a gift—the home that has become the permanent London residence of the prime minister.

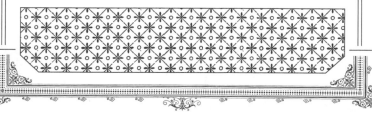

GEORGE II.
Roy d'Angleterre
Né le 30.8.bre 1683.

KING GEORGE II was devoted to his wife, Queen Caroline, but this devotion was not enough to stop him from having a series of mistresses throughout their marriage.

In fact, Caroline was well aware of George's infidelity, and she seemed to take it in stride.

When the queen died, in 1737, the king did not remarry.

He did continue to have affairs, but when he died, he was buried next to his queen at Westminster.

PRINCE FREDERICK, the son of King George II and Queen Caroline, rivalled both his father and his grandfather in scandalous lifestyle.

In fact, both the king and queen publicly made their distaste for their son clear, calling him a monster, a villain, and a rogue.

Frederick did not live long enough to become king, dying nearly a decade before his father.

Instead, King George II was succeeded by Frederick's son, George III.

GEORGE III BECAME KING at the age of 22, determined
to bring a new sense of morality to the royal court, in
sharp contrast to his father.

Duty called on him to take a wife—the German
Princess Charlotte—who would not have been his
first choice, but he nevertheless remained devoted to
her throughout his reign.

Meanwhile, George's brothers and sister kept up the
family tradition of public sexual indiscretion.

To END THE FAMILY TRADITION of impetuous marriages and serial infidelity, King George III proposed making it impossible for royal children to marry without the permission of the king.

The 1772 Royal Marriage Act, however, did not work out quite as he planned. His sons used the law as a shield, blithely proposing to and "marrying" any number of women, secure in the knowledge that their engagements and weddings would be nullified under the law of the land—which was sometimes ironically referred to as an Act for "the Encouragement of Adultery."

As George III aged, mental illness overtook him, and his veneer of morality cracked. He announced he was madly in love with a Countess Elizabeth, whom he referred to as Queen Esther.

He wrote letters to her, expressing his devotion and intentions in embarrassing detail.

The Countess was horrified by the scandal and apparently did not participate in the illicit behavior that was actually taking place only in the demented mind of the king.

STATS

THE LIBRARY OF KING GEORGE III

King George III loved books, and by the time he died, he had collected more than 65,000 of them (plus another 19,000 pamphlets).

The collection includes books printed in Britain, Europe, and North America from the mid-1400s to the early 1800s, and it forms the heart of today's British Library.

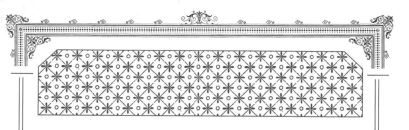

KING GEORGE III'S SON and heir fully restored the royal family's tradition of lascivious and debauched behavior in his youth.

Prince George ultimately pledged himself to Maria Fitzherbert in a phony wedding ceremony.

The marriage was not legal in England for two reasons: the king had not given his royal permission, and the widow Fitzherbert was Catholic.

The Pope, however, gave his blessing and recognized the wedding as legitimate.

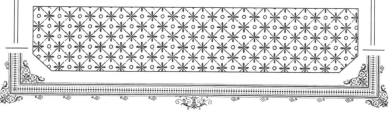

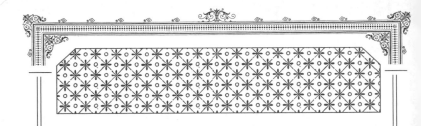

GEORGE PROCLAIMED HIS LOVE for Mrs. Fitzherbert to the end of his life, and she is said to have borne him 10 children.

Nevertheless, he left her to marry (legally) the woman his father chose for him, the Duchess Caroline, after the king promised to pay George's substantial debts.

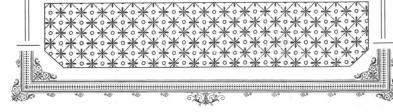

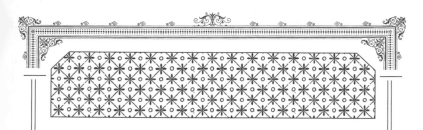

GEORGE AND MRS. FITZHERBERT got back together
when he tired of Caroline and his other mistresses,
but they broke up again later.

Despite the stormy nature of their relationship,
at the end of his life, King George IV named Mrs.
Fitzherbert in his will, and he asked to be buried with
a picture of her around his neck.

WILLIAM, THE THIRD SON of King George III, was
wildly promiscuous in his youth, but in his mid-20s
he settled down and raised a family with an actress.

In their 20 years together, Dorothea Bland (stage
name, Mrs. Jordan) gave William 10 children and
supported him financially.

William abandoned Mrs. Jordan in her 50s, however,
ultimately taking the children and leaving her to die
penniless in France.

DURING THE REIGN OF King George III, Prince William began looking for a wife with whom he could sire a child who might be heir to the throne.

Woman after woman rejected his advances, until a European princess, Adelaide, acquiesced and married Prince William.

They had five children who all died in infancy.

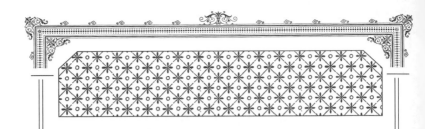

WHEN GEORGE IV DIED without a child eligible to become the monarch, his brother became King William IV, the oldest man ever to become king of England.

He was 64 years, 10 months, and three days old when he took the crown on June 26, 1830.

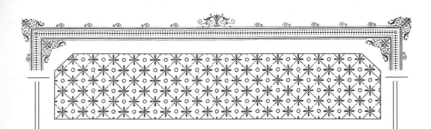

During his short reign, King William IV helped usher in extensive political reforms.

The House of Commons had repeatedly passed laws to extend voter registration to more people, but the House of Lords rejected them all.

The public responded with protests, a bank run, and a tax strike that threatened the peace.

The king ultimately agreed to pack the House of Lords with pro-reform peers to assure the law's passage, but it wasn't necessary.

Opponents backed down in the face of the threat, and the Reform Act of 1832 was passed.

WHICH MONARCH WAS "MOST ANXIOUS TO ENLIST EVERY ONE WHO CAN SPEAK OR WRITE TO JOIN IN CHECKING THIS MAD, WICKED FOLLY OF 'WOMAN'S RIGHTS,' WITH ALL ITS ATTENDANT HORRORS, ON WHICH HER POOR FEEBLE SEX IS BENT, FORGETTING EVERY SENSE OF WOMANLY FEELING AND PROPRIETY"?

   a. Queen Victoria

   b. King George V

   c. King Edward VIII

   d. Queen Elizabeth II

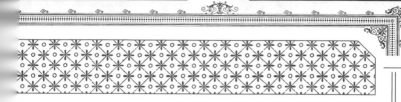

ANSWER: A.

Queen Victoria was vehemently
opposed to efforts to win
women the right to vote,
among other things.

KING WILLIAM IV and Queen Adelaide never produced an heir.

On William IV's death, the crown passed to his niece Victoria, daughter of King George III's youngest son, Edward.

Queen Victoria's reign lasted nearly 64 years, from 1837 to 1901, longer than any other British monarch... so far.

VICTORIA WAS 18 YEARS OLD when she became queen.

A few years later, she married her cousin, Prince Albert of Saxe-Coburg-Gotha.

The marriage lasted 20 years, and they had nine children.

At first, the German Prince Albert was not highly regarded by the British, who thought he had married their queen for the money or the prestige.

Nevertheless, Albert became a British subject and was an influential advisor to his wife and queen, and after they had been married for 17 years, Albert was officially recognized as Prince Consort.

PRINCE ALBERT WAS the leading force behind the Great Exhibition of 1851 in Hyde Park, in which Britain displayed and celebrated its contribution to industrial, artistic, and scientific progress.

He acted as the queen's private secretary and worked to bring issues of social welfare to her attention.

Albert is also credited with interceding to avert what seemed like an inevitable war with the United States in 1861.

Dᴜʀɪɴɢ ᴛʜᴇ U.S. Cɪᴠɪʟ Wᴀʀ, an American ship intercepted and boarded the *Trent*, a British ship carrying two Confederate emissaries to England.

In what the British viewed as a highly provocative and illegal act, the Americans took the Confederates prisoner.

British politicians drafted a response that amounted to an ultimatum to be delivered to the United States and began preparations for a global military conflict.

Prince Albert suggested rewording the message to allow the Americans to apologize and to return the Confederate emissaries, which is what ultimately happened.

Queen Victoria oversaw Great Britain during a period of tremendous technological, political, and social change.

The Victorian Era, as it has become known, saw the growth of a British Empire that spanned the world.

Queen Victoria was the leader of the world's most powerful nation through a period of relative peace and prosperity.

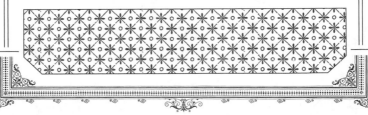

STATS

THE SUN NEVER SET ON THE
BRITISH EMPIRE

The British Isles cover about 122,000 square miles.

During the reign of Queen Victoria, however, the British Empire stretched over more than 14,000,000 square miles—more than one fifth of the world's land mass.

The number of people under British rule was equally astounding—more than 458 million—about one fourth of the world's population.

PRINCE ALBERT DIED suddenly of typhoid fever in 1861 at the age of 42.

Queen Victoria was devastated and mourned the loss of her love for the rest of her life.

Victoria continued to meet her responsibilities as head of state, but she withdrew from public life almost completely.

Her absence made her unpopular with her subjects, but as she slowly began to return to the public eye in the late 1860s, her public image improved.

TECHNOLOGICAL ADVANCES of the 19th century in communications, transportation, and photography helped Queen Victoria to be seen by more of her subjects than ever before possible.

They also made it possible for her subjects to make eight different attempts on her life between 1840 and 1882.

Although the law still called for drawing and quartering anyone who attempted to kill the queen, juries no longer had a taste for such brutality.

As a result, new rules were implemented to treat mentally deranged criminals more mercifully.

CONTEMPLATING THE NUMEROUS unsuccessful attempts on the life of Queen Victoria, Prime Minister William Gladstone considered it a positive sign that the men who tried were so incredibly inept.

In other countries, he said, assassins were more competent, but in England, no one in his right mind would want to kill the queen.

After the last attempt, Victoria herself weighed the risks of making public appearances and decided, "It is worth being shot at to see how much one is loved."

In 1877, Victoria was made Empress of India, in addition to ruling over Canada, Australia, New Zealand, and a substantial portion of Africa.

When she died in 1901, she was both the oldest and longest-reigning British monarch in history.

Queen Elizabeth II beat Victoria's record as the oldest monarch on December 20, 2007, when she became older than 81 years, seven months, and 29 days.

POP QUIZ

WHO WAS THE FIRST BRITISH MONARCH TO VISIT THE UNITED STATES?

a. Queen Victoria in 1855

b. King George V in 1911

c. King George VI in 1939

d. Queen Elizabeth II in 1976

ANSWER: C.

King George VI crossed the
Canadian–U.S. border at
Niagara Falls, then went on
to visit New York City and
Washington, DC, to encourage
the United States to become
involved in the conflict that
became World War II.

THE HOUSE *of* WINDSOR
(née Saxe-Coburg-Gotha)

MONARCH	YEARS *of* REIGN
Edward VII	1901–1910
George V	1910–1936
Edward VIII	1936 (abdicated)
George VI	1936–1952
Elizabeth II	1952–present

Elizabeth II

By marriage, Queen Victoria was a Saxe-Coburg, but genetically, she was of the House of Hanover, and those leaders had the dubious distinction of finding their first-born children detestable.

George I despised George II.

George II hated Fredrick.

George III found George IV contemptible.

In keeping with her heritage, Victoria said of her son Edward, "I never can, or ever shall look at him without a shudder."

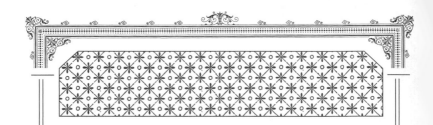

QUEEN VICTORIA'S SON Edward was a disappointment to her from the beginning:

"Handsome I cannot think him, with that painfully small and narrow head, those immense features and total want of chin."

And when she and Albert found out that he was having sex with an Irish actress while in the army, at the age of 19, Prince Albert went to have a long talk with the boy.

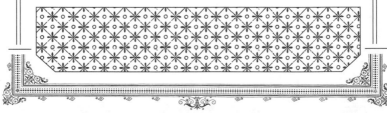

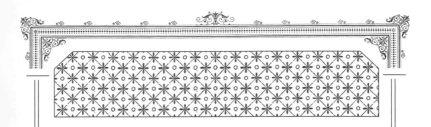

When Albert returned from his father–son chat with Edward at Cambridge, the Prince Consort was seriously ill with typhoid.

In a matter of weeks, he was dead.

Victoria blamed Edward and never forgave him.

Meanwhile, Edward continued living the lifestyle his mother found so distasteful.

She, in turn, refused to allow him access to any government documents or to train him in any way to take over from her upon her death.

EDWARD VII SPENT MOST of his life as Prince of Wales, waiting for the moment when he would be king.

He became well known for his eating, drinking, gambling, and being an all-around playboy.

He finally ascended to the throne in 1901, becoming the epitome of a 20th-century monarch.

In contrast to his mother, who had been a recluse for decades, King Edward VII became a very public figure, traveling and spending time with his subjects.

AN INCOMPLETE LIST *of* THE FAMOUS
MISTRESSES IN THE LIFE OF KING EDWARD VII

- Lillie Langtry, actress

- Sarah Bernhardt, actress

- Lady Randolph Churchill, mother of Winston

- Alice Keppel, great-grandmother of Camilla, Duchess of Cornwall

- Countess of Warwick, "Daisy" Greville, the inspiration for the old song "Bicycle Built for Two"

- Giulia Barucci, self-proclaimed greatest prostitute in the world

- Agnes Keyser, philanthropist and humanitarian

Sarah Bernhardt

KING EDWARD VII spoke German and French and was known as the Uncle of Europe, because he was related to most of the royals on the continent.

He is credited with helping to bring about the Entente Cordiale of 1904, a treaty of political friendship with France that set the stage for the alliances that would dominate 20th-century Europe.

KING GEORGE V came to power in 1910, in the midst of a political showdown.

For the first time in two centuries, the House of Lords had vetoed a budget from the House of Commons.

Conservative Lords objected to the unprecedented taxes and new social spending that would redistribute Britain's wealth.

The House of Commons responded with a bill to limit the Lords' legislative power.

King George V intervened by threatening to pack the House of Lords with Liberals, causing a dramatic shift of power.

The Conservatives backed down before that could happen, and the new budget passed.

KING GEORGE V and his wife, Queen Mary, visited India in 1911—the only such visit by a King-Emperor.

When World War I broke out, he made hundreds of visits to troops in the field and in hospitals, advocated for humane treatment of prisoners, and for the rights of conscientious objectors.

He also decided it was time to change the family name.

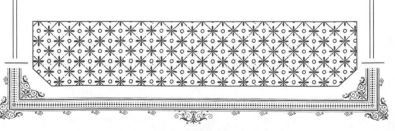

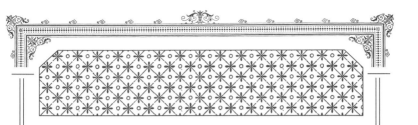

IN RESPONSE TO the anti-German sentiment riding high in Great Britain because of World War I, King George V decided that Saxe-Coburg-Gotha wasn't a politically correct name for an English monarch.

He changed his family name to Windsor, and the House of Windsor has ruled Great Britain ever since.

At the same time, King George V also ruled that only the sons of a brother of the king would be given the titles "Prince" and "Royal Highness."

Their children would be treated like non-royal English dukes.

In 1936, when George V lay dying of cancer and there was no hope of recovery, his physician met with the king's wife and son to discuss a most delicate topic: euthanasia.

The main concern was that the king might not die in time to be the next day's headline in the London *Times*.

Fearing that the news would be published first in the less prestigious afternoon papers, everyone agreed the doctor should give the king a shot of cocaine and morphine to hasten his death.

And he did.

As Prince of Wales during the reign of his father, George V, Edward VIII was a flamboyant, social, and rambunctious young man who spent most of his time enjoying the privileges of his rank, just like most of his ancestors.

But with Edward, there was an unexpected twist—he fell in love and wanted to get married.

THE WOMAN OF EDWARD VIII's dreams was a remarried American divorcée, and simply having her as a mistress was not enough for either of them.

She was willing to divorce again to be free to marry Edward, and he wanted to marry her.

It was a shocking prospect at the time. As leader of the Church of England, Edward's marriage to a woman with two living ex-husbands would have been unacceptably scandalous.

EDWARD VIII BECAME KING immediately upon the death of his father, but he was never crowned.

Instead, he abdicated—the first and only British sovereign to do so voluntarily—in order to be with the woman he loved.

His brother became King George VI and named Edward VIII the Duke of Windsor.

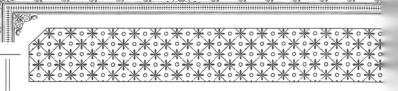

POP QUIZ

IF KING EDWARD VIII HAD NOT ABDICATED, WHO WOULD BE THE BRITISH MONARCH TODAY?

    a. Prince Michael of Kent

    b. Prince Richard, Duke of Gloucester

    c. Princess Alexandra, Countess of Snowdon

    d. Queen Elizabeth II

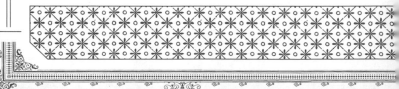

ANSWER: D.

Queen Elizabeth II would have been next in line to the throne when her uncle Edward died in 1972.

By making Edward VIII a duke after his abdication, King George VI restricted him from running for office or speaking on political issues in Parliament.

Edward and his wife spent the rest of their lives as celebrities in quasi-exile, but they remained controversial.

Not only did Edward publicly express pro-Nazi, racist, and anti-Semitic positions, but also recently released documents suggest he was always looking for a way to return to power.

In fact, there is evidence that Hitler intended to return Edward to the British throne if the Nazis had defeated England.

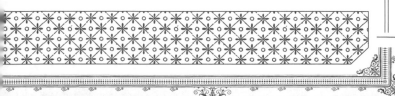

King George VI saw his empire through World War II, remaining in Buckingham Palace even as German bombs fell around him.

His steady reserve and public appearances throughout the war and the difficult post-war period made him popular with his subjects.

His daughter, Queen Elizabeth II, ascended to the throne on his death in 1952, at the age of 25.

STATS

QUEEN ELIZABETH II,
RECORDING INDUSTRY IMPRESARIA

Queen Elizabeth II is the first member of the royal family to be awarded a gold disc from the recording industry.

During the Queen's Golden Jubilee in 2002, a pop concert was held at the Buckingham Palace Garden, attracting some of the biggest names in modern music.

EMI produced a CD of the event, called the "Party at the Palace," and it sold 100,000 copies within the first week of release.

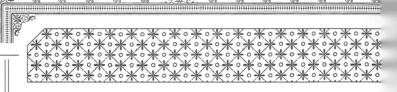

POP QUIZ

WHICH OF THE FOLLOWING IS NOT TRUE ABOUT QUEEN ELIZABETH II'S WEDDING CAKE?

a. Prince Philip cut the 9-foot-tall, 500-pound cake with his sword after the ceremony.

b. The "10,000-mile wedding cake" got its name because the ingredients came from Australia and South Africa.

c. A piece of the cake sold at auction in 2013 for 560 pounds Sterling, which is about $840 (US).

d. The same recipe was used for the wedding cake of Prince William and Kate Middleton.

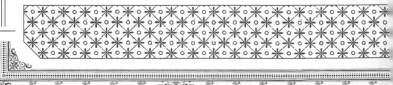

ANSWER: D.

The Duke and Duchess of
Cambridge's cake was also
traditional fruitcake, however
not the same recipe as
Queen Elizabeth II's.

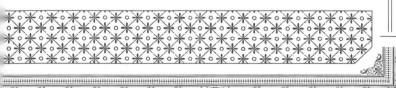

Queen Elizabeth II trained as a truck driver and mechanic during World War II.

She became an active member of the Women's Auxiliary Territorial Service in February 1945 and made it to the rank of Honorary Junior Commander.

Other titles she held at the time included Patrol Leader of the Buckingham Palace Girlguides, as well as Colonel-in-Chief of the Grenadier Guards.

THE ROYAL FAMILIES of England take their swans very seriously.

In the 12th century, when swans were considered delicious, the monarch reserved ownership of all unmarked Mute Swans (which, incidentally, are not really mute at all).

Today, the queen exercises ownership rights only on the swans of the Thames River.

A bird census called "Swan Upping" takes place every July, when the "Royal Swan Warden" and the "Royal Swan Marker" travel upriver, counting and marking and making sure the birds are safe.

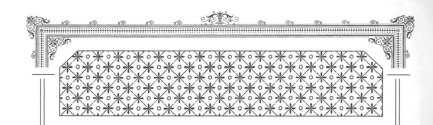

Under a statute from 1324, which is still valid today, the queen owns all the sturgeons, whales, and dolphins—the "Fishes Royal"—in the waters around the UK.

When captured within three miles of UK shores, or washed ashore either dead or alive, they may be claimed on behalf of the Crown.

It has been speculated that, back in the day, the king reserved the whalebone for the queen's corsets and stays.

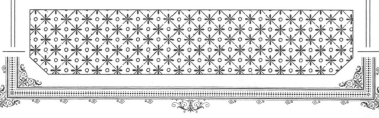

STATS

ROYAL BEE HIVES

In spring 2009, two Italian honeybee hives were placed on a five-acre island in the middle of the garden at Buckingham Palace. The bees have access to more than 350 varieties of wildflowers and 600 plants from the hives' secluded position. After the first year the two hives had produced 83 jars of honey. In spring 2010, two more hives were added on the island.

STATS

WHAT'S THE QUEEN WORTH?

Two different valuation organizations have estimated the net worth of Queen Elizabeth II to be about $500 million, not including the value of the assets she holds in the national trust.

Some of her personal holdings include stud farms, a fruit farm, and one of the world's largest stamp collections, started by her grandfather, King George V.

STATS

GIFTS TO THE QUEEN FROM HER SUBJECTS ON THE OCCASION OF HER DIAMOND JUBILEE

436 books

235 CDs and DVDs

81 pieces of embroidery or knitting

78 self-portraits

40 digital photograph books

28 wall hangings

19 tea towels

9 jigsaw puzzles

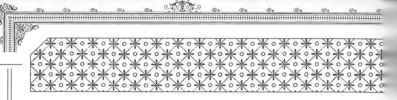

POP QUIZ

QUEEN ELIZABETH II HAS MET EVERY U.S. PRESIDENT
DURING HER REIGN EXCEPT ONE. WHICH PRESIDENT DID
SHE NOT MEET?

a. John Kennedy

b. Lyndon Johnson

c. Richard Nixon

d. Gerald Ford

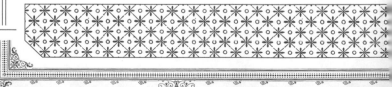

ANSWER: B.

Beginning with Harry Truman,
Queen Elizabeth II has met
every U.S. president except
Lyndon Johnson.

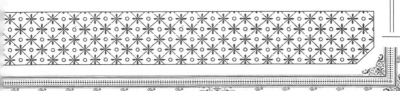

If…

If Queen Elizabeth lives until mid-September 2013…

And…

If Prince Charles outlives her…

Then…

When he ascends to the throne, he will be the oldest person ever to become king of England.

The current record-holder is King William IV, who was king for almost seven years.

And, if Queen Elizabeth lives until September 9, 2015, she will exceed Queen Victoria's record as the longest reigning British monarch.

QUEEN ELIZABETH II'S 12 PRIME MINISTERS

Winston Churchill	1951–55
Sir Anthony Eden	1955–57
Harold Macmillan	1957–63
Sir Alec Douglas-Home	1963–64
Harold Wilson	1964–70
Edward Heath	1970–74
Harold Wilson	1974–76
James Callaghan	1976–79
Margaret Thatcher	1979–90
John Major	1990–97
Tony Blair	1997–2007
Gordon Brown	2007–2010
David Cameron	2010–present

WHEN PRINCE CHARLES married Camilla Bowles, she officially became the Princess of Wales, but you can just call her Duchess.

Camilla, Duchess of Cornwall, decided not to take the Princess title, out of respect for the public's lingering love for Charles's first wife, Diana.

She may also forgo being crowned queen, if and when Charles becomes king.

If she does, Camilla will be, simply, HRH The Princess Consort.

THE LINE *of* SUCCESSION TO THE BRITISH CROWN

QUEEN ELIZABETH II

Charles, Prince of Wales

Prince William, Duke of Cambridge

Henry, Prince of Wales

Prince Andrew, Duke of York

Princess Beatrice of York

Princess Eugenie of York

Prince Edward, Earl of Wessex (THIRD SON OF THE QUEEN)

Viscount Severn (SON OF THE EARL OF WESSEX)

The Lady Louise Mountbatten-Windsor
(DAUGHTER OF THE EARL OF WESSEX)

Anne, the Princess Royal (ONLY DAUGHTER OF THE QUEEN)

Mr. Peter Phillips (ONLY SON OF THE PRINCESS ROYAL)

Miss Savannah Phillips
(ELDER DAUGHTER OF PETER AND AUTUMN PHILLIPS)

Miss Isla Phillips
(SECOND DAUGHTER OF PETER AND AUTUMN PHILLIPS)

Mrs. Michael Tindall (DAUGHTER OF THE PRINCESS ROYAL)

Viscount Linley (SON OF THE LATE PRINCESS MARGARET)

The Hon. Charles Armstrong-Jones
  (SON OF VISCOUNT LINLEY)

The Hon. Margarita Armstrong-Jones
  (DAUGHTER OF VISCOUNT LINLEY)

The Lady Sarah Chatto
  (DAUGHTER OF THE LATE PRINCESS MARGARET)

Mr. Samuel Chatto (ELDER SON OF LADY SARAH CHATTO)

Master Arthur Chatto
  (SECOND SON OF LADY SARAH CHATTO)

Prince Richard, Duke of Gloucester
  (THE QUEEN'S FIRST COUSIN)

Alexander, Earl of Ulster
  (SON OF THE DUKE OF GLOUCESTER)

Lord Culloden (SON OF EARL OF ULSTER)

The Lady Cosima Windsor
  (DAUGHTER OF THE EARL OF ULSTER)

The Lady Davina Lewis
  (ELDER DAUGHTER OF THE DUKE OF GLOUCESTER)

Miss Senna Lewis (ONLY CHILD OF LADY DAVINA LEWIS)

The Lady Rose Gilman
  (SECOND DAUGHTER OF THE DUKE OF GLOUCESTER)

Miss Lyla Gilman (ONLY CHILD OF LADY ROSE GILMAN)

Prince Edward, Duke of Kent
(FIRST COUSIN OF THE QUEEN)

The Lady Amelia Windsor
(YOUNGER GRANDDAUGHTER OF THE DUKE OF KENT)

The Lady Helen Taylor
(DAUGHTER OF THE DUKE OF KENT)

Mr. Columbus Taylor

Master Cassius Taylor

Miss Eloise Taylor

Miss Estella Taylor

The Hon. Albert Windsor

The Hon. Leopold Windsor

The Lord Frederick Windsor

The Lady Gabriella Windsor

Princess Alexandra, the Hon. Lady Ogilvy

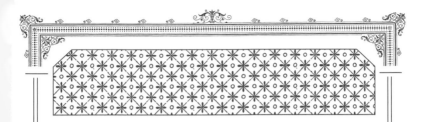

BRITISH SCHOOLCHILDREN learn this poem to help
them remember the lineage of monarchs from William
the Conqueror to the present day:

> *Willie, Willie, Harry, Stee,*
> *Harry, Dick, John, Harry three;*
> *One, two, three, Neds; Richard two,*
> *Harrys four, five, six... then who?*
> *Edwards four, five; Dick the bad;*
> *Harrys (twain), Ned six (the lad);*
> *Mary, Bessie, James, you ken;*
> *Then Charlie, Charlie, James again...*
> *Will and Mary, Anna Gloria,*
> *Georges four, Will four, Victoria;*
> *Edward seven next, and then*
> *Came George the fifth in nineteen ten;*
> *Ned the eighth soon abdicated;*
> *Then George six was coroneted;*
> *After which, Elizabeth*
> *And that's all folks until her death.*

Where will the first child of
William and Kate, the Duke and
Duchess of Cambridge, fit into
the line of succession?

At first, that child will be third in
line, between Prince William and
Prince Henry.

Because of the rules of
primogeniture, what happens next
will depend, among other things, on whether they have
a boy or a girl.

What is primogeniture?

Put simply, primogeniture puts brothers in front of sisters when it comes to inheritance. For example, Anne, Princess Royal, was the second child of Queen Elizabeth II, but she comes after her younger brothers on the current list of succession.

If the child of William and Kate is a boy, he will be third in line, period.

If it's a girl, she will be third in line, unless she someday has a brother.

Doesn't anybody think that's inappropriate for this day and age?

 There is talk about doing away with primogeniture *and* changing several of the other rules of succession in an effort to bring the monarchy in step with current day sensibilities.

For example, some think that marrying a Roman Catholic should not mean automatic exclusion from the line of succession—something originally put into place because the monarch is also the head of the Church of England.

Is the monarch prohibited from marrying anyone other than a Catholic?

No. The rules of succession only specifically forbid marriage to a Catholic.

That's not because the Parliament of 1701 thought being Catholic was worse than being Jewish, Moslem, Hindu, or anything else.

On the contrary, marriage of a would-be monarch to someone of a non-Christian faith was so unthinkable as to make it unnecessary to create a rule about it.

Why doesn't the queen just change the rules?

 The queen doesn't have the authority. The rules of succession were put in place by Parliament with the Bill of Rights (1688) and the Act of Settlement (1701).

Those laws are interpreted to mean that...

- the sovereign rules through Parliament,

- succession to the throne can be regulated by Parliament, and

- a sovereign can be deprived of his title through misgovernment.

What would it take to change the rules of succession today?

Queen Elizabeth is the monarch of 16 individual realms, including the United Kingdom.

Each of those realms (mostly former colonies) has a say in the rules of succession, and it can be very complicated.

In Canada, for example, there is a question as to whether, in addition to Parliament, the provinces must also unanimously approve of any changes to the rules of succession to the Canadian throne.

STATS

THE ROYAL FAMILY, BY THE NUMBERS

- ◆ 3,000 public and charity organizations list a member of the royal family as either a patron or president.

- ◆ 2,000 official engagements are carried out by the royal family each year, in the UK and overseas.

- ◆ 70,000 people are entertained each year at dinners, lunches, receptions, and garden parties at the royal residences.

- ◆ 100,000 letters are received and answered each year by the royal family.

What is the best way to
keep informed about the day-
to-day activities of the British
royal family?

 If you have access to the Internet,
you can take your pick: The British
monarchy has had a website since
1997, a YouTube channel since
2007, a Twitter feed since 2009,
and both Flickr and Facebook pages since 2010.

What happens to a commoner
who makes a mistake in addressing
a member of the royal family?

Not much.

The days of "Off with his head!" are long gone.

But it *is* more polite if you follow the traditional forms:

Instead of shaking hands, men should bow their heads only, and women can do a small curtsy.

When first addressing the queen, call her "Your Majesty."

Others in the royal family are addressed at first as "Your Royal Highness."

After that, "Ma'am" or "Sir" will do in conversation.

What are the traditional forms of addressing royalty in letters?

 "Sir" or "Madam" are fine ways to start.

If you want, you can begin with "Your Majesty" or "Your Royal Highness."

Concluding with "Yours sincerely" is always nice.

But if you want to go all the way when writing to the queen, you can end with, "I have the honour to be, Madam, Your Majesty's humble and obedient servant."

OFFICIAL MAILING ADDRESSES
OF MEMBERS *of* THE ROYAL FAMILY

The Queen

Buckingham Palace

London SW1A 1AA

The Prince of Wales and The Duchess of Cornwall

Clarence House

London SW1A 1BA

His Royal Highness The Duke of Edinburgh

Buckingham Palace

London SW1A 1AA

His Royal Highness The Duke of York

Buckingham Palace

London SW1A 1AA

Their Royal Highnesses The Earl and Countess of Wessex

Bagshot Park

Bagshot

Surrey GU19 5PL

Her Royal Highness The Princess Royal

Buckingham Palace

London SW1A 1AA

Their Royal Highnesses The Duke and Duchess of Gloucester

Kensington Palace

London W8 4PU

His Royal Highness The Duke of Kent

St. James's Palace

London SW1A 1BQ

Her Royal Highness The Duchess of Kent

Wren House

Palace Green

London W8 4PY

ABOUT THE WRITER

VICTOR DORFF does not believe he has a drop of royal blood in his veins (or anywhere else). As an American lawyer living in London years ago, he studied the British system of constitutional monarchy with amazement. Even today, he marvels at the persistence of the royal family and the role it plays in the governing of so many people in so many different lands. So far in life, Dorff has worn many hats—educator, inventor, entrepreneur, network news producer—but he has not given up hope that someday his collection of headgear will include a crown.

Art Credits

Depositphotos.com: Alexandr Blinov, 160; © daksel, 184; © Anatoliy Gosudarev, 112; Sergey Goryachev, 134; Patrick Guénette, 16 (seal), 17, 36, 40, 49, 90, 181; Sergey Kohl, 21, 74, 171; Georgios Kollidas, 16 (portrait), 27, 35, 55, 58, 68, 72, 79, 104, 106, 119, 136, 148, 150, 164; neftali77, 191; © pavalena, 14; © Laschon Richard, 12; © S-E-R-G-O, 92

iStockphoto.com: Ivan Burmistrov, 180; Classix, 39, 107, 109, 127, 152, 155; Ralf Hettler, 165; HultonArchive, 128; Constance McGuire, 138; © mecaleha, 22; Linda Steward, 122; traveller1116, 77; Duncan Walker, 32, 33, 44, 53, 56, 78, 82, 91, 129, 151

Shutterstock.com: © Denis Barbulat, 28; © Betacam-SP, 166; Bocman1973, 43; Brendan Howard, 176; lynea, 143, 157; © Jane Rix, 62

Pepin Press: 1, 2, 5, 57, 183